MW00446457

THE SCARECROW BOOK

JAMES GIBLIN & DALE FERGUSON

CROWN PUBLISHERS, INC., NEW YORK

ACKNOWLEDGMENTS: We want to thank the following institutions and individuals who helped us track down facts and photographs for the book: the Orientalia Division, the Prints and Photographs Division, and the American Folklife Center of the Library of Congress; the National Agricultural Library, U. S. Department of Agriculture; the Library of the Museum of the American Indian, Heye Foundation; the New York Public Library and its Picture Collection; the Massachusetts Horticultural Society Library; the Old Sturbridge Village Library; the Chicago Museum of Science and Industry; the Museum of American Folk Art; Plimouth Plantation; the School of Food and Natural Resources and the Slavic Languages Department, University of Massachusetts; the Hadley Farm Museum; the Ely Farm Library; the Norfolk Rural Life Museum; Somerset House, Ltd.; the W. Atlee Burpee Company.

Paula J. Fleming, the National Museum of Natural History, Smithsonian Institution; Kathy Rose, the Photographic Collection, American Museum of Natural History; John Rousseau, Natureworks, Inc.; Crispin Gill, Editor, *The Countryman;* Don Yoder, Editor, *Pennsylvania Folklife;* Gerald E. Parsons, Archive of Folk Song, the Library of Congress; Jim Cope; Maishe Dickman; Ruthe M. Ferguson; Barbara Grosset; Richard B. Newton; Jeanne Prahl; and Sondra Radosh.

We especially want to thank Mr. Senji Kataoka of Tokyo, Japan, who sent us a beautiful selection from the more than three thousand photographs he has taken of Japanese scarecrows.   — THE AUTHORS

10 9 8 7 6 5 4 3 2

Frontispiece: Newlywed scarecrows, *Rachel Ritchie/Boston Globe*
Illustrations on pages 48–51 by Susan Detrich

The text of this book is set in 14 pt. Garamond Book.
The illustrations are black-and-white photographs.

Library of Congress Cataloging in Publication Data
Giblin, James.   The scarecrow book.   Summary: Discusses the many different types of scarecrows farmers in various parts of the world have used over the past 3000 years to protect their crops. 1. Scarecrows – Juvenile literature. [1. Scarecrows] I. Ferguson, Dale, joint author. II. Title. SB996.C6G53 1980   632'.68   80-13800
ISBN: 0-517-53862-8

For Ann and Kelley and Norma Jean
— J.G.

For my mother
— D.F.

THE SCARECROW BOOK

The French called it "the terrifier."

The Zuni Indians named it "the watcher of the corn sprouts."

We call it a scarecrow.

When we think of a scarecrow, we usually think of a figure that looks like a man or a woman, standing in the middle of a field. But over the centuries, people have used many different kinds of scarecrows to protect their crops. Some were noisemakers that rattled and banged. Others were pieces of cloth that waved in the wind, or metal objects that shone in the sun. Some scarecrows were dead birds. Others were live men and boys.

Ever since people began to grow grain, crows and other birds have been a danger to the crops. An attack by a flock of

hungry birds might mean that a farmer would lose so much corn or wheat that he and his family would starve during the long winter months. To prevent that from happening, farmers of long ago began to make scarecrows.

Scientists have not found any of those early scarecrows, but they know they existed because people drew or wrote about them, and their pictures and words have survived. From these we know that some ancient peoples believed scarecrows had special powers. The Greeks believed a scarecrow god protected their gardens, and they carved wooden statues of him. The Japanese believed scarecrows could see everything that was going on around them.

This book describes these and many other scarecrows that farmers in different parts of the world have used over the centuries.

Egyptian farmers scaring birds
away from a field
Wall painting from the tomb of Nakht.
Metropolitan Museum of Art,
photograph by Egyptian expedition

The oldest scarecrows we know of were made along the Nile River more than three thousand years ago. To protect their wheat fields from the flocks of quail that flew over them every autumn on their way south, Egyptian farmers built rectangular wooden frames, put them in the middle of the fields and covered them with fine nets. Then the farmers wound long white scarves around their own bodies and hid at the edge of the fields to wait for the quail.

As soon as the quail appeared, the farmers ran into the fields, waving their scarves and shouting. This frightened the quail so much that many of them landed on the nets, where their feet became caught in the fine mesh. The farmers stuffed the quail into sacks and took them home. Besides protecting the crops with these scarecrows, the farmers and their families had a fine quail dinner.

Figure of a young man resembling
Priapus, from ancient Italy
Cleveland Museum of Art,
Sundry Purchase Fund

The first scarecrows that looked like people were probably the wooden statues made by farmers in Greece more than twenty-five hundred years ago.

The Greeks believed that a god named Priapus helped them protect their wheat fields and the grapes in their vineyards, and they told many stories, or myths, about him. In one myth, he was the ugly son of a handsome god named Dionysus and a beautiful goddess named Aphrodite. Because Priapus was such a homely baby, his mother left him on a hillside to die. Fortunately he was discovered by some vineyard keepers, who took him home with them.

When Priapus was eight or nine, he often played in the vineyards. The keepers noticed that crows and other birds stayed away from the grapes when Priapus was there, and they decided that the birds were frightened by the boy's ugly face and twisted body. The keepers encouraged him to come to the vineyards every day, and at harvesttime they gathered in more grapes than ever before.

The news of how Priapus had protected the grapes soon spread all over Greece. Some farmers thought that statues that looked like Priapus might keep the birds away from their grapes and wheat, so they carved wooden statues of him, painted them purple and stood them in their fields. Sure enough, the birds stayed away, and in the fall the farmers harvested bigger crops than ever. As more and more Greek farmers carved statues of Priapus, he became known as the god of gardens.

We do not know how much of this myth is true, but we do know that Greek farmers carved statues of Priapus and used them as scarecrows. Usually a club was put in one of the statue's hands and a sickle in the other. The club made the statue look more dangerous, and the sickle was supposed to help ensure a good harvest.

At harvesttime there was a celebration, and Greek farmers put sheaves of newly cut grain and piles of grapes beside the statues of Priapus to thank him for protecting the crops.

The Romans copied many Greek customs, and they, too, carved figures of Priapus and put them in their fields.

When Roman armies occupied what is now France, Germany and England, they brought Roman customs with them, including a belief in Priapus. So wooden statues of him appeared in the fields and gardens of those countries, and farmers continued to use them even after the fall of the Roman Empire in A.D. 476.

At the same time the Greeks and Romans were using statues of Priapus to guard their crops, Japanese farmers were making other kinds of scarecrows to protect their fields of rice.

From the time the Japanese began to grow rice, almost twenty-five hundred years ago, every plant has been precious because only twenty percent of Japan's terrain is suitable for farming. To protect their crops, Japanese farmers often hung old rags and meat or fish bones from sticks placed in the middle of their fields. Then they set the sticks on fire. The burning rags and bones smelled so bad that birds and small animals stayed away.

The Japanese called this kind of scarecrow a *kakashi*, which means something that has a bad smell. At first the word was used only for scarecrows made of rags, bones and sticks. But later the Japanese started calling all scarecrows kakashis, whether they smelled bad or not.

There were several different kinds of kakashi in ancient Japan, but all of them were built on tall bamboo poles. Rice grows best in four to six inches of water, and during the three-month growing season the poles soaked up the water without rotting.

Some kakashis were bamboo sticks hung from wooden boards that were placed on slender poles in the fields. When the wind blew, the boards swayed and the bamboo sticks clattered together, scaring the crows and sparrows away.

Other kakashis were colored streamers of cloth or shiny pieces of metal and glass that were tied on ropes. Farmers strung the ropes from poles around the field. When the streamers blew in the wind and the glass or metal objects flashed in the sun, the birds stayed away from the rice plants.

Japanese farmers also made kakashis that looked like people. This kind of scarecrow had a wooden frame and was often stuffed with straw. It was dressed in typical Japanese farming clothes: a round straw hat that rose to a peak in the middle, and a raincoat made of reeds. A bow and arrow were often placed in its arms to make it look more threatening.

Like the Greeks, the Japanese thought that one of their gods helped to protect the crops. The god's name was Sohodo-no-kami, which means protector of the fields. The Japanese believed that the spirit of Sohodo-no-kami left his home in the mountains every spring, came down to their farms

Japanese scarecrow holding
a bow and arrow
Senji Kataoka

and entered the kakashis that looked like people. His spirit stayed in the kakashis all summer long, watching over the rice plants as they grew.

Because birds flew so close to the kakashis and sometimes landed on them, Japanese farmers thought the birds told their secrets to the god's spirit. "Though his legs do not walk, he knows everything under heaven," a Japanese farmer would often say of his scarecrow.

At the beginning of the harvest in late September, Japanese farmers offered freshly cut stalks of rice to the scarecrows. This was their way of thanking Sohodo-no-kami for protecting the crops.

After the harvest, in mid-October, the farmers believed that it was time for the spirit of Sohodo-no-kami to return to his home in the mountains. The farmers brought all the scarecrows in from the fields, put them in a great pile and surrounded the pile with special rice cakes for the god to eat on his journey home. Then they lit the scarecrows with a torch and burned them. This ceremony was called "the ascent of the scarecrow."

The following spring, Japanese farmers would make new kakashis for the spirit of Sohodo-no-kami to enter.

Japanese scarecrow dressed
in the traditional reed raincoat
Senji Kataoka

Like Japanese farmers, European farmers in the Middle Ages believed their scarecrows had special powers, and many superstitions grew up around them. In Italy, farmers placed the skulls of animals on the tops of tall poles in the fields. They thought the skulls would drive away both birds and diseases harmful to the crops.

In Germany, farmers made figures of witches out of wood and carried them out to the fields at the end of winter. The farmers believed the witches would draw the evil spirit of winter up into their bodies, so that spring could come. The witches also served as scarecrows and helped to keep crows away from the newly planted seeds of wheat and oats.

According to a very old German story, scarecrows were even used to frighten people. In the story a small German kingdom, threatened with attack by a powerful neighbor, gathered all the wooden scarecrows from miles around and lined them up on the field of battle. When the enemy saw the figures from a distance, they thought they were soldiers and, believing they were outnumbered, they fled. The people of the small kingdom celebrated their "victory," and then carried the scarecrows back to the fields.

While the scarecrows in Germany and some other European countries were made of wood, in medieval Britain scarecrows were boys of nine, ten and older.

These boys were called bird scarers or bird shooers, and they were usually the sons of peasants. The land the peasants farmed was owned by a lord or other landowner, and part of the peasants' crop had to be given to the landowner as payment for the use of the land. The peasants were allowed to keep the rest of the crop for themselves and their families to live on.

In the 1300s the boy bird scarers patrolled the wheat fields carrying bags of pebbles and small stones. When any crows or starlings appeared, the boys would run after them, waving their arms and throwing stones. As they ran they would sometimes shout, "Crow, crow, get out of my sight, or else I'll eat thy liver and light [lung]."

All summer long the bird scarers watched over the fields

from dawn to dark, in good weather and bad. To help pass the time, they made slingshots and had contests to see who could hit the most fence posts as well as birds.

Then in 1348 the Great Plague struck Britain. The disease killed almost half of the population. Landowners had to find other ways to protect their crops. Some surrounded their fields with piles of thorny brush to keep the birds from landing. Others stuffed a sack with straw, carved a face out of a turnip or a gourd and made a scarecrow that they stood against a pole. They hoped the scarecrow would make the birds think a boy was guarding the field.

On farms where there were still a few boys to act as bird scarers, each boy had to patrol three or four acres by himself. Some bird scarers were only seven years old, and a few were girls. These bird scarers did not carry bags of stones; instead they carried clappers made of two or three pieces of wood joined together at one end.

Wooden clappers used by
British birdscarers
Norfolk Museums Service,
Great Britain (Rural Life Museum)

The clappers enabled the bird scarers to guard the fields more carefully and easily. A stone drove away only one or two birds at a time, but the loud noise of the clappers scared off entire flocks.

As a bird scarer walked through the fields and banged his clappers, he often sang this song:

> *Away, away, away, birds,*
> *Take a little bit and come another day, birds.*
> *Great birds, little birds, pigeons and crows,*
> *I'll up with my clappers and down she goes!*

The bird scarers built rough shelters of sticks and dirt to stay in when wind or rain swept through the fields. They brought their dinners with them in cloth bags, and sometimes sang this lullaby when they settled down for a meal or to rest:

Flee away, blackie cap, don't ye hurt my master's crop,
While I fill my tatie-trap [mouth], and lie me down to
take a nap.

Many British boys and girls were proud of being bird scarers and spent their winter evenings carving new clappers for the next season's work.

Bird scarers continued to patrol British farms for hundreds of years. Then in the early 1800s new factories and mines opened up all over Britain and many of the bird scarers left to take better-paying jobs in them. They were replaced in British fields by human-looking scarecrows, just like the ones we see on farms today.

Indian tribes in North America in the 1600s and earlier depended on corn for food. The Pueblos, who lived in a dry region of the Southwest, said: "Without water, there is no corn. Without corn, we die."

To protect their crops, Indian tribes in all parts of North America used scarecrows of one kind or another. They also used bird scarers. But unlike the bird scarers in Britain, most of the Indian bird scarers were grown men.

In the area that is now Virginia and North Carolina, Indian bird scarers sat on raised wooden platforms at the side of the cornfields. Roofs of woven straw sheltered the men from the sun and the rain. When they saw a crow or a woodchuck approaching the corn, the men would howl or shout at it until it fled.

In Georgia, entire families of Creek Indians were selected by their chiefs to watch over the tribe's cornfields. When spring came, the families left their village and moved into huts built in the grassy spaces between the fields so they would be close to the growing corn. They lived there all summer and took turns protecting the crop from birds and other pests. After the corn was harvested in the fall, they moved back to the village for the winter.

The Seneca Indians, who lived in what is now New York State, soaked corn seeds in a poisonous herb mixture and scattered them over the fields. When a crow ate one of these poisoned seeds, it would become dizzy and fly crazily around the field, scaring away other birds.

In the American Southwest, the lands of the Zuni Indians were so crowded with crows that the Zunis invented many different kinds of scarecrows.

Zuni children in the late 1800s even had contests to see who could make the most unusual scarecrow. A white man who lived among the Zunis once saw an old woman scarecrow that the children had made. She had a basket on her back, and a rattle in her hand that was made from a dog's rib, a tin can and a stick. When the wind blew, the rattle clacked and clattered and scared away the crows.

The man also saw a male scarecrow with outstretched arms and long gray hair made from a horse's tail. The scarecrow's face was a piece of black rawhide, with a hole at the bottom for the mouth. A huge tongue made from a red rag hung loosely from the mouth and swung back and forth in the wind.

The Zunis called their human-looking scarecrows "the

watchers of the corn sprouts." But they didn't keep all the crows and ravens away, so the Zunis built another kind of scarecrow.

Cedar poles were placed about six or nine feet apart all over a cornfield. A bunch of thorny leaves was tied around the top of each pole so birds could not land there. Cords made from fibers of the yucca plant were then strung from pole to pole, forming a sort of giant clothesline that ran back and forth across the field. Tattered rags, pieces of dog and coyote skins and the shoulder blades of animals were hung from the lines. The sight of the rags waving in the wind and the sound of the bones clacking against each other kept most birds away.

But some birds were not stopped by either "the watchers of the corn sprouts" or the yucca lines, so the Zunis also set little rope nooses in the ground between the corn plants. Every day the Zunis gathered up the birds whose legs had been caught in these nooses and carried them home, where they were starved to death.

When a bird was dead, the Zunis sewed its body to a cross made out of two twigs. Then they hung it upside down, with its wings outstretched, from one of the yucca lines. The Zunis believed that the sight and smell of the dead crow would scare off other crows if nothing else did.

The Navajos, too, hung the bodies of dead crows on poles to frighten away other birds. And like many Indians in Virginia and North Carolina, some Navajo men acted as bird scarers. The Navajos also made scarecrows that looked like people, and sometimes they simply tied a bunch of rags to a stick, hoping that the birds would fly away when the rags waved in the wind.

One Navajo scarecrow seen by a traveler in the 1930s was completely original. It was a toy teddy bear fastened to the top of a pole! The old Navajo woman who made it claimed it did a very good job of protecting her crop.

Dead crow hanging
from a stick
Robert Doisneau/Rapho

In the 1600s, people from Europe began to settle in North America. Among the first settlers were the Pilgrims, who came from England and landed in Massachusetts in 1620.

The Pilgrims learned about Indian corn, a crop that they had never raised in England, from Squanto, a Pawtuxet Indian living in Massachusetts. Squanto showed the Pilgrims how to plant corn by putting two or three seeds in a small mound of earth and adding a dead herring for fertilizer. Then he made another mound of seeds and fish a foot or so away, and then another, until there was a row.

The Pilgrims often put extra seeds in the mounds. They thought this would ensure that at least some of the seeds would survive raids by hungry crows. As they planted the seeds, the Pilgrim farmers would often say:

One for the cutworm,
One for the crow,
One for the blackbird,
And three to grow.

To protect the corn as it grew, the Pilgrims stood guard in the fields like the bird scarers in their native England. Often all the members of a family, from the youngest to the oldest, would take turns guarding the field from morning till night.

Crows weren't the only creatures that threatened the crop. Wolves dug up the fish that were buried with the corn seeds at the beginning of the season. The biggest and strongest bird scarer in the family kept watch on spring nights when wolves were most likely to creep into the fields. If a wolf appeared, the bird scarer would yell or throw rocks and clubs at it. As a last resort, he might fire a gun, if he had one.

More and more people settled in America in the 1700s, and more land was cleared for farming. Larger fields were created, and a family could no longer afford to spend so much time guarding the crops. Even the children were needed for other jobs.

To replace bird scarers, some farmers made human-looking scarecrows stuffed with straw and put them in their fields. Like the scarecrows in Britain after the Plague, these were usually dressed in old clothes and had turnips or large gourds for their heads.

Other farmers tied strings hung with bright pieces of cloth around their fields, as did the farmers in ancient Japan. Still others covered corn seeds with tar so the birds couldn't reach the kernels inside. But when the sprouts broke through the coating, the birds often pulled them up and ate the seeds.

By the early 1700s many more American farmers had guns, which they sometimes fired in their fields to scare crows and other birds away. Some farmers believed that the mere smell of gunpowder would frighten the crows, so they sprinkled gunpowder on their fields. But usually it didn't work.

As the population of the American colonies grew, the people needed more and more grain. None of the methods farmers had used to protect their fields had been completely successful. Many farmers finally decided that the only way to keep crows away from their crops was to shoot them.

By 1750 towns all up and down the Atlantic coast offered

payments, called *bounties,* for dead crows. These bounties drew young boys, eager for target practice and pocket money, into the fields after school. The boys were a new and deadly kind of bird scarer. They brought in dead crows by the basketful.

In Massachusetts, a boy could earn a shilling — worth about what a dollar is worth now — for each crow he killed. In Pennsylvania, the bounty was three pence for each crow or each dozen blackbirds. Pennsylvania residents even sent a petition to the General Assembly in 1754, asking it to pass a law requiring each new settler in the state to kill at least twelve crows.

By the middle of the 1800s so many crows had been killed that birds were less of a threat. But this created an unexpected problem. Corn borers and other worms and insects, which the birds had once eaten, were now destroying more corn and wheat than the crows had. Scientists then urged farmers to stop killing the crows.

Throughout the country, town meetings were held in

which people argued for and against the killing of crows. Most farmers came to believe that if the crows really served a useful purpose, they should be allowed to live. After the meetings, many towns stopped offering bounty payments for dead crows and went back to using scarecrows.

Soon building a scarecrow became a spring ritual on many small American farms. In some places, neighboring families competed to see who could make the most colorful and unusual scarecrow. While the children gathered old clothing to dress it, the farmer and his wife made the frame.

Immigrants who came to the United States from Europe in the nineteeth century brought with them their own superstitions about crows and their own ideas of how to make scarecrows.

In Pennsylvania, many farmers from Germany, who were known as the Pennsylvania Dutch, thought that every kernel of seed corn should be passed through the hole in a beef bone before it was planted. These farmers believed this would keep the seeds from being eaten by birds.

When a Pennsylvania Dutch farmer planted his seed, he often dug three holes in a corner of the field. In the first hole

Nineteenth-century farmers harvesting wheat, with scarecrow in background
Engraving from "The Song of the Sower" by William Cullen Bryant

he put three kernels of corn for the birds, in the second three kernels for the worms and in the third three kernels for the bugs. He hoped that the birds, worms and bugs would eat the seeds he had planted for them and leave all the others he sowed alone.

Like the farmers in New England, Pennsylvania Dutch farmers believed that the smell of gunpowder would keep crows away from a field. They greased wooden shingles with fat and dusted them with gunpowder. Then they hung the shingles from strings tied to stakes and set the stakes among the rows of corn. When the wind blew, the shingles turned around on the strings and the smell of gunpowder spread all over the field.

The Pennsylvania Dutch also built a human-looking scarecrow, which they called *bootzamon,* or bogeyman. Like most other American scarecrows, the bootzamon's body was a wooden cross. Its head was made of a broom or mop top, or a cloth bundle stuffed with straw.

The bootzamon was usually dressed in a pair of old, torn overalls or trousers, a long-sleeved shirt or coat and a battered woolen or straw hat. Often a large red handkerchief was tied around its neck to cover the place where the head was fastened to the body.

Sometimes a second scarecrow was put at the opposite end of the field or garden. It was called *bootzafraw,* or bogeywife, and it was dressed in a woman's long dress or coat. A sunbonnet was often placed on its head.

Many Pennsylvania Dutch farmers believed that the bootzafraw kept the bootzamon company and helped him to protect the corn. They were also used to guard strawberry patches and cherry orchards.

A bootzamon or bootzafraw might even be found near a chicken coop. If a mother crow saw newly hatched chicks in a coop, she was likely to snatch one up and carry it back to her nest to feed her own young. Farmers believed a bootzamon or a bootzafraw would prevent this from happening.

In the twentieth century, scarecrows have been especially popular in bad times. During the Great Depression, in the 1930s, American farmers used scarecrows to protect their small fields of corn and wheat. Some hung dead crows from poles as the Zuni Indians did. Others tied pieces of white cloth to strings and strung them around their fields as the farmers of ancient Japan did.

In America and Europe after World War II, many small farms were combined to make larger ones. Farmers bought more tractors, harvesters and other kinds of mechanized equipment, and agriculture became a big business.

These postwar farmers had little faith in the old-fashioned scarecrow. In 1947 a British magazine asked more than a hundred farmers, "Do scarecrows scare birds?" Fewer than half replied yes.

In place of scarecrows, many farmers began to use poisonous chemicals like DDT to protect their crops. When

A scarecrow from North Carolina
in the 1930s
Dorothea Lange/Library of Congress

insects or birds ate something that had been covered with one of these chemicals, they died very quickly.

By the 1950s the use of such poisons in the United States was widespread. Farmers dipped seeds in chemicals before they planted them, and then as the crops grew they dusted or sprayed them with chemicals. On very large farms, planes flew low over the fields, spraying acre after acre of corn and wheat with DDT and other chemicals.

Then, in the early 1960s, scientists discovered that these chemicals didn't break down quickly enough into nonpoisonous substances. They feared that the chemicals might remain on the crops and ultimately poison the people who ate them.

By the late 1960s people began asking for foods that had been grown without agricultural chemicals. Many farmers stopped using them and sought other ways to protect their crops.

Some farmers, like their fathers and grandfathers, tied miles of strings hung with pie plates or tin cans around their fields. Others used whirligigs that spun in the air like small windmills and startled birds and animals.

In Britain, a fireworks company invented an "automatic crop protector." This was a metal box with three arms that was placed on top of a pole. Connected to the box was a rope containing caps that exploded every forty-five minutes. Whenever one of the caps exploded, the three metal arms flapped up and down, making a loud clatter. The noise and flash of the explosion, followed by the clash of the metal arms, was guaranteed to scare away animals and birds. It also scared any people who happened to be passing by.

In some areas, small planes that had once sprayed chemicals on crops were equipped with noisemaking machines. They flew over large cornfields and drove away crows and other birds. The only problem with this bird-scaring device was that the noise sometimes made birds fly down into the corn rather than away from it.

(Left) British fireworks scarecrow
Illustrated London News
(Below) Modern scarecrow made
of metal reflectors
Natureworks, Inc.

On other farms, huge funnel-shaped light traps were used to protect the crops. At night the strong spotlights behind the funnels were turned on. Birds blinded by the lights flew down into the funnels and were trapped in cages at the bottom. The farmers let most of the birds go free, but killed the crows and other birds that threatened their crops.

One farmer in New England trapped about twenty crows by chasing them into a corner of the field where he had spread some seed in a burlap net. He made a tape recording of their cawing and then let the birds go. The next day he put the tape recorder out in his cornfield and turned it up to full volume. The sounds of the terrified crows kept other birds away better than anything else the farmer had ever tried!

Farmers and gardeners still use human-looking scarecrows today. There are even ready-made ones for sale. A large seed company offers an inflatable vinyl model that flaps its arms and legs in the wind.

Inflated scarecrow made of vinyl
W. Atlee Burpee Co.

Most people who use scarecrows prefer to make their own, though. Homemade scarecrows can be found on small country farms, in suburban vegetable gardens and in city community gardens. One city gardener, when asked if scarecrows scared birds, said he wasn't sure if they did or not. But he knew that at night thirty or so scarecrows on an acre of land did a good job of keeping thieves out of the garden.

Human-looking scarecrows guard fields and gardens in Britain, France, China and Japan, as well as the United States. Many are stuffed with straw and wear worn-out clothes like the scarecrows of long ago. But others are dressed in blue jeans instead of wool trousers, have heads made of plastic bottles, and wear wigs instead of sunbonnets.

Live bird scarers are also used today. In India and some Arab countries, old men sit in chairs at the edge of the fields and throw stones at attacking birds. And in the spring of 1979

Modern Japanese scarecrow
Senji Kataoka

British scientists at a plant-breeding institute advertised for a bird scarer after other devices had failed to keep birds away from their experimental crops.

The job paid the equivalent of $2.40 an hour and the bird scarer had to start work at 4:00 A.M. From then until nightfall he would walk up and down through the ten-acre cornfield and wave his arms to scare away the crows and rooks that were eating the seeds.

The job would last for about three weeks, until the corn plants were too big for the birds to pull up. Then the bird scarer wouldn't be needed again until late summer, when the corn ripened. At that time the birds would return, and once more the bird scarer would have to drive them away.

As long as birds are a threat to their crops, farmers all over the world will continue to use scarecrows of one kind or another, just as they have for the past three thousand years.

A Scarecrow for Your Garden

The directions that follow tell you how to build a small scarecrow, about 5 feet tall, suitable for low-growing vegetables such as lettuce and radishes. It will probably be easier to make if an older brother or sister, or your father or mother, helps you.

YOU WILL NEED:

- A 1-inch-by-3-inch wooden board, 6 feet long. This will be the spine of your scarecrow. Try to have it sawed to a point at one end by the lumber dealer.

- Another 1-inch-by-3-inch board, 2 feet long. This will be your scarecrow's arms.

- A hammer and some 1½-inch nails.

- Whatever clothes you choose — worn-out jeans and a flannel shirt, or an old skirt and a blouse.

- Two or three pieces of string or yarn, long enough to wrap around the scarecrow's waist and neck.

- An old white pillowcase.

- A bundle of straw, a small pile of dry leaves, a package of cotton or synthetic batting or a bunch of rags.

- Colored pencils, wax crayons or waterproof paints.

- A shovel.

- Some pebbles or small stones.

- Whatever finishing touches you choose — a hat, a shawl, a baseball cap.

DIRECTIONS:

1. Gather all the materials you'll need and bring them to a place where you will not damage the floor, and where you'll have enough room to lay your scarecrow out flat. Put old newspapers on the floor.

2. Put the shorter piece of wood across the 6-foot piece of wood in the form of a cross. Center the shorter piece about 12 inches from the top of the longer piece, and nail the two pieces together with three or four nails.

3. If you're dressing your scarecrow in pants, put one leg of the pants over the bottom of the longer piece of wood and pull up the pants – the other leg will hang free. Or you can stuff both legs with straw. If you're dressing the scarecrow in a skirt, put the skirt around the longer piece of wood and pull it up. Don't pull either the pants or the skirt all the way up to the piece of wood that will be the

scarecrow's arms. You'll want to leave room for the shirt or blouse.

4. Put a shirt or blouse over the scarecrow's arms, and tuck it into the pants or skirt. If the shirt has buttons, button them up. Then tie the waist securely with a piece of yarn or string.

5. Stuff the pillowcase with the straw, leaves, batting or rags. This will be your scarecrow's head. Give it a round shape, and then flatten one side. This side will be your scarecrow's face.

    Slip the open end of the pillowcase over the top of the scarecrow's "spine" — the long piece of wood — and tie it in place securely with string. Be sure to keep the flatter side of the head facing you.

6. With the pencils, crayons or paints, draw in the eyes, nose and mouth of your scarecrow's face, using as few lines as possible. The simpler the facial features are, the farther away you'll be able to see them.

7. When the face is dry, your scarecrow will be ready for the garden. After you've chosen the right spot and the scarecrow has been carried out to it, dig a narrow hole about 9 inches deep. Put the scarecrow in place, and pack the hole

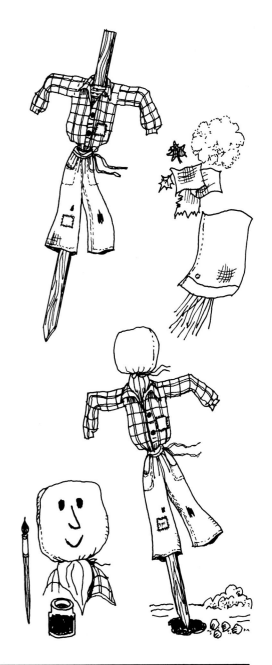

with dirt and stones so that the scarecrow will stand straight. If you can, have someone help you by holding the scarecrow in place while you fill in the hole.

8. Now you can add some finishing touches to your scarecrow's costume. You may want to put an old baseball cap or stocking cap on its head, or a broad-brimmed cowboy hat. Or you may decide your scarecrow would look nice in a wig or a brightly colored bandanna or a black hat with a veil.

   At the end of each arm you can hang tinfoil pie plates that will shine in the sun and clatter in the wind. Or maybe you'd like to pin a pair of mittens or old gardening gloves to the ends of the sleeves to make hands for your scarecrow.

9. It's a good idea to check up on your scarecrow during the summer, especially after a storm. If it's wobbly, you may have to pack more dirt and rocks around it to make sure that it remains standing.

10. When the summer is over and your crop is harvested, carry your scarecrow inside the garage or barn. Next summer, you can dress the frame in fresh clothes and make a new head and face for it.

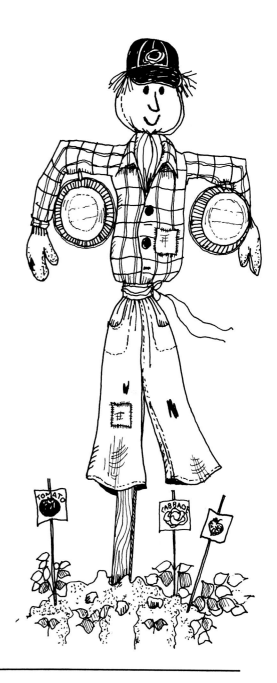

Bibliography

Baker, Margaret. *Folklore and Customs of Rural England.* London: David and Charles Ltd., 1974.

Crevecoeur, Michel Guillaume St. Jean de. *Sketches of Eighteenth-Century America.* New Haven: Yale University Press, 1925.

Cushing, Frank Hamilton. *Zuni Breadstuff.* New York: Museum of the American Indian, Heye Foundation, 1920.

Doisneau, Robert. *Epouvantables Epouvantails.* Paris: Editions Hors Mesure, 1965.

Encyclopedia of Superstitions, Folklore and the Occult Sciences of the World. Chicago: Yewdale and Sons, 1903.

Fried, Fred and Mary. *America's Forgotten Folk Arts.* New York: Pantheon, 1978.

Gras, Norman Scott Brien. *A History of Agriculture in Europe and America.* New York: F. S. Crofts, 1940.

Graves, Robert. *The Greek Myths.* Vol. 1. New York: Penguin Books, 1960.

Hand, Wayland, D., ed. *Popular Beliefs and Superstitions from North Carolina.* Durham: Duke University Press, 1964.

Hawkins, Benjamin. *A Sketch of the Creek Country.* Atlanta: Georgia Historical Society, 1848.

Herbert, Jean. *Shinto at the Fountainhead of Japan.* New York: Stein and Day, 1967.

Hill, Willard Williams. *The Agricultural and Hunting Methods of the Navajo Indians.* New Haven: Yale University Press, 1938.

Howe, George and Harrer, G. A. *A Handbook of Classical Mythology.* New York: Gale Research, 1970.

Joya, Moku. *Things Japanese.* Tokyo: Tokyo News Service Ltd., 1960.

Long, Amos, Jr. "Dutch Country Scarecrows," in *Pennsylvania Folklife,* Fall 1961.

Mangelsdorf, Paul Christoph, and Reeves, R. G. *The Origin of Indian Corn and Its Relatives.* College Station: Agricultural and Mechanical College of Texas, 1939.

Montet, Pierre. *Everyday Life in Egypt in the Days of Rameses the Great.* Translated by A. R. Maxwell-Hyslop and Margaret S. Drower. New York: St. Martin's Press, 1958.

Parker, Arthur Caswell. *Iroquois Uses of Maize and Other Food Plants.* Albany: University of the State of New York, 1910.

Rutman, Darrett Bruce. *Husbandmen of Plymouth: Farms and Villages in the Old Colony 1620-1692.* Boston: Beacon Press, 1967.

Index

Date Due

JUL 7 '87				

Giblin, James
AUTHOR

Scarecrow Book, The
TITLE

Mar. '85   J632

DATE DUE	BORROWER'S NAME
JUL 7 '87	

Giblin...Scarecrow Book, The......J632

OLIVE WARNER MEMORIAL
LIBRARY